A House of Publishing Anthology

A Collection of

120 Best Poems

by Best 10 Writers

Volume 10

Authors:

Parita Bheda | Riya Kulkarni | Varsha Shailesh Bhosale (Ehsaas)
Shalini Lakshman Rao | Muzaina Tasneem
Shubham Sawant | Swapnadip Bhattacharya
Manasi Manchanda | Anlet Nevi J | Sara Mhatre

Title: **A Collection of 120 Best Poems by Best 10 Writers**

Authors:

Parita Bheda | Riya Kulkarni | Varsha Shailesh Bhosale (Ehsaas)
Shalini Lakshman Rao | Muzaina Tasneem | Shubham Sawant
Swapnadip Bhattacharya | Manasi Manchanda | Anlet Nevi J | Sara Mhatre

First Published by Manda Publishers in 2024

ISBN: 978-93-6402-793-9

Price in INR: 249/-
House of Publishing
An imprint of Manda Publishers
www. mandapublishers.com
publishat.hop@gmail.com
+91 9999190496

Cover Design: Garima
Typography: Charchit

Distributed by:
Amazon, Flipkart, Manda Publishers etc.

Printer:
Manipal Technologies Ltd.
Noida

Writers

Parita Bheda

Verses are the portals of your mind, translated into reality. I aim to expand this power on to paper and open new doors to such different portals. The beauty of writing is to traverse into that particular portal of the writer into thinking what might be the writer's reality for writing it?
My name is Parita Bheda and I love to express this power of poetry. I am a teacher, writer, philanthropist and a poet. I enjoy writing about some unique yet universal experiences of different people through the lenses of my life. I find success when the reader finds comfort in my writings. It's a rare art to identify these emotions, so I love that readers find the answers through my poems. I wish to impact more lives with a sense of positivity.
I would love to get feedbacks and views for my poetry from my dear readers.
My email id: bhedaparita1@gmail.com

Always Remember These Nights

As you walk through this doorway,
Holding a smile, to rainbows from grey,
In the corner of your heart, as you summon the demons like a knight,
Always remember these nights,

Through the sounds joining your celebration,
Give a thought, while in your misery, did they give you an invitation?
Behold the souls, uniting against your every plight,
So always remember these nights,

Before you accept that ring from a charming smile,
Take a look at the withered rose that they threw, leaving you hostile,
Now when your tears couldn't water those petals, under the moonlight,
While the allure of success, makes the hope reignite,
remember these nights.

Remember these nights, always remember nights,
How was your fall? Before this height,
The hands who lent you a cloth, while you were drenched in sorrow,
The souls who kindled the hope, when you had no sight of tomorrow

Always remember that night,
When you picked up the strength from dark to light,
When you wrote your destiny, while the infinity showed more sunsets,
So always remember that night, that your story never ended with a regret.

The Love of My Dreams

The night is young, swaying through your dreams,
I got no shoulder but your sombre dreams,
I should have waited for another dance,
You took me heaving with a mystical trance,
I long for the feeling of your raunchy arms,
It ought to be broken but I drown in your charms,
It's a dusty feeling as we go through our abode
An affinity for those grey walls, that lit up as you uphold,
The casting of my soul through the swirls of your passion,
The look you give me as you gorge in seclusion,
Evenings and nights, fragrant as you astound,
However, the bond slipped with another enticing beat that you found,
Affections are millions but a golden touch is hard to receive,
The show through falling garbs might deceive,
My love, don't let such a stalling, steal you from our little world,
Yes, we danced together in the next universe till our feet turned cold.

The Air of Fresh Start

Golden rays shone in front of my feet,
A new path has started manifesting,
Small steps of courage, I got to greet,
I removed those pebbles of dilemma, which were pesting,

My thoughts dance in a new rhythm,
While the warmth of those rays makes me feel safe,
Boundaries that let my ambitions chafe,
Sing merrily as petals of lilies blossom,

I still dread the unknown,
But now I am not alone,
I have myself and my dreams,
I move forward with a new gleam,

It's a melancholy of emotions,
But I stick strongly to notions,
It is what it makes me,
Through something that cannot shake me,

I held to perspectives of differences by others for longer,
But flowing into the shape that I am truly makes me stronger,
Meadows call out the hymns of fragrance,
They would have never bloomed out with thoughts of stagnance.

The Beauty of The First Date

We wandered through streets with farms,
Within a thousand faces of strangers, I felt solace in your arms,
We ran a bit, laughed a bit, and somewhere stumbled, just like our bond,
However tough the roads got, we never stopped our way to search what was beyond,

Beyond, we found a lake, with weeds clustered,
As the sparrows through their nests muttered,
The alchemy grew as I drowned deep in your eyes with the serine waves,
The sun began shedding its light touching the last of its rays on us as a wave,

We captured moments of joy as our young love bloomed,
Though treachery of faith demanded separation, as smoke gloomed,
Our love-struck the beats of the heart and dusted the sombre shades,
Tinges of grey flew with the color of merriment, as my hands on your shoulder were laid,
I crave every bit of the evening with lilies brighter and water benevolent,
Your warmth adored me to a safe heaven as I held you tight, though you were silent,
You got lost in my smile, while I couldn't take my eyes off yours,
I still can't take off those memories all over me, feeling the way you adore,

Arms in arms, hours melted in those comforting lips,
The way you never wanted to leave me for a moment as you tighten your grip,
I walk again through that memory lane with the sweet essence of your affection,
We are still holding our hands and locking our lips, in the lake's reflection.

The Beauty of Time-Space

We live a hundred lives in a life, some lessons and some blissful chapters,
Some are bookmarks and some take us somewhere or maybe nowhere,
After every small tale, a new present is born,
Pretty little accidents or some thorns,
The roadways expands and freezes a memory of the old present,
Creating the new one's crescent,
Memories do get older, we become colder or grateful,
However enjoy the feeling of your present,
Life becomes about all those moments
That were beautiful,
The feeling of a new hello, still finds the traces in the fluttering heart of old blushes,
Their laughter and love is still alive in that present, with which your cheek flushes,
This way present is a cycle keeping each memory immortal,
Each memory of each time space stays infinite, maybe in your mind's portal.

Life: A confectionery

Ever gazed the confectionery's sweet goodies?
The cakes, pies and the mouth-watering candies,
With such a delicacy crafted and baked,
With such love and sweetness life is made!

God, the confectioner has given such a treat,
Given to the spirit with a human outfit,
Sometimes bitter like dark chocolate but sweet,
Also sweet moments like strawberries come with a big greet.

It brings chills at times as ice sparkles on cream,
How much ever we feel the pain of sensitivity,
The taste is only enjoyed by the witty!
So my friend, lets live and love life under its sweet beam.

Golden Day Rises Once

Each one's life is a definition of success,
So each one has a new day blessed,
In which we progress and express
ourselves,
Getting the biggest victory in beating your failures
yourselves,
And adding every book of experience in your life's shelves.

Such a golden day rises once,
Full of golden opportunities achieved by your brilliance,
While their sweet results keep tinkling in your ears,
Such a feast of happiness expressing with years,
You keep hearing and let lose your fears,

But you would wonder when will this day arrive?
For this day how much I have to strive?
The day may be today or tomorrow my friend,
Each day is blank so make it a new brand!

You would think this day is best,
But you would realize the second day is greater than first
The golden day achieving crave,
Will make you sweet intelligent and brave,
So instead of a golden day a golden life is paved.

Deepest wounds unearthed

In the benevolence of night a heart rendering thunder occurred,
It shook my consciousness until a squeaky cry into my ears entered,
All the way amidst the spooky cemetery I wandered,
I thought to meet a phantom in white coloured,
Instead an alluring appearance from nowhere appeared,
I was hypnotized as his charm splendored,
That shook me away till the bottom of my heart and my speech slurred,
He approached for my hand before I would have muttered,
Curling his hand around "I was waiting for you" he muttered,
I danced with him the whole night without getting tired,
The bliss of happiness made me forget about the cemetery that I always feared,
In that serenity of moment, suddenly a gun fired!
His shiny clothes were blood stained and my vision blurred,
I gained conscious at my house with red flowers on my bed embroidered,
My brain jerked with an unidentified memory that I remembered,
The forgotten memory with the same boy that was injured,
With those memories a joy within me ushered.

That One Guy with Glasses

Burning flames of desires,
I don't know what this time conspires?
Swirled around an exuberance of emotions,
Solitude felt lonely because of that one constellation,
Constellation deep within the thousand depths of those eyes,
Hypnotizing me to a world where innocence dies,
All that remains is the thirst to explore deeper,
As the mountain of our desire grows steeper,
A stance through that alchemy is enough for my adversity,
Fortunate enough that his glasses, guard my sanity.

Chasing the Last Strings of Love

Doors of heaven shone in front of me,
I found light among thee,
I ran through canopies and orchids,
I dove into my heart's deepest beads,
Shaped more rhymes staring hours,
Through the existence that my heart craves,
I can't explain how much for it I made tours,
You don't know how hard this hit as my destiny waves,
A crippled existence of my faith,
Some darkest deeds of philanthropy I made for this haith,
Redeem all my sins through the pain,
But almighty don't grab this Shane,
Shed upon all the cosmic energy,
I lay upon your feet like the clergy,
The sparkle of his eyes touched my corpse, alive,
Different allure of his innocence pulls all the knives that were shived,
Days of mourn storm away with his sight,
I will not let his hand slip away with all my might,
Rewrite my history, rewrite my possibility,
As I shun such a probability,
Of a success devouring away his warmth,
All the boons, all my soulful deeds here I put forth,
I am no human without this mercy,
To be with the one I fancy,
Weigh each deed down by pulling the threads of our faith together,
Entwine us as two different lines into one letter,
Pay heed to this yearning,
As it's the last chance for your angel from hell to return.

The Night Became Darker

Traffic lights got blurry,
Echoes screamed in my mind's quarry,
Through all the emotions I burry,

Raindrops that splattered hard on my car,
Slowly turned into tears, revealing my scars,
I just remembered pain had broken all the bars,

I was like the dusk and you were the dawn,
We were just destiny's pawns,
I clutched you tight as the night took me away from the horizon's lawn,

I got the darkest night in my share,
Uniting for that tiniest moment, though poles apart is all that I care,
Two lover's hearts got a beautiful tear,

Our worlds are different but I want to step in your universe,
Oh! I forgot about the true love's curse,
Although it hit me the worse,

You found warmth in the flickering light,
While I got the lonely and frosty night,
If you could hold my hand once tight, I would have made our love reach new heights,

Now we are two souls apart, but share the same flame,
Faith showed how the largest of flames can be tamed under it's name,
Now the universe won't be the same, what a shame!

It has always been the case,
Time overpowers the last of the love's trace,
I don't understand, why did the universe made my heart race?

For your beautiful flickering light in the first place,
What a cruelty! Now my soul longs your warm embrace,
Questions and questions ran through my mind that why wasn't love a beautiful lace?

However that lace twisted and turned to my blurry vision that night,
Splatters of blood from the lover's heart could be seen through the blurry red lights,
I gripped my steering with all the pain tight,

I was still drowned in the anonymity of past,
Soon the horns rang with the engine's blast,
I drove in a hurry through the dark shadows my dead love cast.

I Want to Go Back

I want to go back love, I want to go back,
To that beautiful bench, you stuck flowers in my hair,
To those pristine waters of the summer evening lying with you on the deck,
Laughing and giggling on the old town clock's stairs,

Take me back love to all our pretty dates,
As the places become prettier with our love,
Ohh my god! Look how your smile radiates!
Should I send some more love letters with a dove?

You made me your hopeless romantic,
Your love made me that cute little lunatic,
I stumble reminiscing how your hands rolled over my waist,
Ahh! those lips with a lasting taste,

I want to be friends with the rain,
As I want to dance with you on that quaint lane,
Where the cherry blossoms await to sprawl,
Oh! Still our names are engraved on the lane's walls,

Mosses try to hide that heart,
But they forget that's my lover's art,
Even the faith started overpowering our forever,
But it does not know we are stronger than ever,

The places might not have our souls dancing to their tunes,
But they hold the love borrowed from our laughter,
Don't worry pretty we will be back soon,
Open a whole new chapter,

Don't chain the beads of distance as separation dear,
We have endless years of forever,
Just take my hand and swirl me around,
Even though our roads might not be bound,

Although our sun of forever is yet to soar,
Dear, always remember the places still speak our tales as their folklore.

Riya Kulkarni

Hello, I'm Riya Kulkarni, an 18-year-old aspiring author studying in 12th standard with a passion for writing poems and stories. I love to write poems and stories based on human emotions. It speaks about young love, exploring its beauty, friendship and challenges through compelling narratives. With talent for understanding the human heart, I craft narratives which resonate with the readers of all ages. Writing has always been my way of understanding the world and connecting with others. I am very much passionate about learning and understanding the beauty of human emotions. I'm thrilled to share my journey and stories with you. I hope you will love my writing and would also love to hear your feedbacks.

My email id is- author.riya19@gmail.com

A Girl I Know

I know a girl,
Who's just like a beautiful pearl,
Hair without curl,
She's beautiful,
And supercool

I met her recently,
But felt a connection instantly,
She's like a flowing river,
She's a beautiful picture,
She's a glitter,
With amazing sparkle,
There's a spark in her,
And she'll shine forever

Once you talk to her,
You get to know her,
She's a girl with pure heart
She's a girl who's like a fine art

Her madness cures u,
Her talkative nature entertains u,
Her smile heals u,
And she always teaches you,
Something new

She's a friend,
That everyone needs,
She's a friend,
Who'll always be there for u,
She's a friend,
Who'll always stand by ur side,
She's a person,
That everyone wants to be

I am glad,
To call her my friend,

I am glad,
To know her,
I am glad,
To have her

Having a friend like her,
Is a pure blessing,
Life without her,
Is very blur,
When u meet her,
Your heart starts melting,
And writing about her,
Is never ending!

A Dancing Man

He saw an old man dancing alone on the beach. He went near him and asked,

"Why are you dancing, sir?"
The old man smiled and said, "I am going to meet the love of my life very soon. "The man laughed and said, "At this age?"

"Yes, I am going to meet her after a long time!"
They both sat on the sand.

"The first time I saw her, I knew she's the one. I remember her looking at me with those beautiful, blue eyes. I still remember the golden, silky hair of hers. When I close my eyes, I remember all the moments spent together.

Whenever I open a book to read. I find the flowers she gifted to me. When I look at the morning sun, I remember her bright smile; I remember her laugh. When I see this calm sea, I remember us, getting lost into each other's eyes.

My every single day, is incomplete without missing her. And I

know, she too misses me a lot.

I am just afraid of one thing."

"What is it?" the young man asked.

"I don't know whether she'll recognize me or not; Afterall, it's been a long time and I have changed a lot in past twenty-five years since then, we haven't met each other."

"Don't worry sir, she will definitely recognize you"

The old man stood up and started dancing again. Seeing at his happiness, the young man too started dancing with him.

While dancing, he asked:

"She's so lucky to have you. Where is she right now?"

The old man smiled and pointed towards the dark sky.

Aankhein

Baatein jo dil mein chupi reheti hain,
Aankhein woh sab kehe hi deti hain

Baatein ankahi,
Aakhein bayaan karhi deti hain

Jhoot chahe jitna bhi bolo,
Aankhein sach bata hi deti hain

Nazre chahe kitni bhi churalo,
Aankhein wapis nazre mila hi leti hain

Aakhon mein chipi hain bohot saari baatein,
Aur Basi hain bite palon ki yaadien,

Kabhi padho in aankhon ko,
To jaano woh ankahi dastaan,
Kyunki,

Baatein jo dil me chupi rehti hain,
Aankhein vo sab keh hi deti hain..

Falling For Your Smile

When I close my eyes,
I don't know how,
The time flies'
I just spend time,
Looking at you and your smile

When I close my eyes,
I always see you,
Looking at me,
With those beautiful eyes,
And that's how the whole flashback starts

I remember the times,
When I felt low,
You were always,
The first one to know,
I remember the efforts,
You took to make me feel better,
That's what makes you
Even more special.....

I then remember,
All the happy times,
That we spent together,
Chatting and laughing,
Clapping and dancing,
Whenever I looked at you,
You were already staring,
Like you had your whole world,
In front of you

I noticed you,
Every single time,
I looked for you,
Every single day,
I wanted to meet you,
Everyday,

I wanted to be with you,
Forever and,
I wanted you,
To lock your eyes with mine
Once again....

I love the way,
Your eyes and your smile,
Conveyed your feelings to me,
Every time,
They had something new to say

Sometimes,
They were talking to me
Sometimes,
They were lifting me,
Sometimes,
They were playing with me,
And sometimes,
They were innocently flirting with me

Every time we talked,
I felt something,
I felt the connection,
I felt our bond,
I felt the affection,

I thought I was being weird,
I thought I was acting different,
I thought something was wrong with me,
Maybe I was very confused,

But,
I wanted us to be more than friends,
I wanted you to shine,
I wanted you to be only mine,
To be honest,
I didn't knew what exactly I wanted,
Until I realized,
That I was falling for your smile...!

She Fell First

She fell first
But he fell harder,
She fell for his sharp eyes,
But he fell for her teary eyes
She fell for his cold smile,
But he fell for her silly laugh,

She fell for his wet lips,
But he fell for her red cracked lips,
She fell for his perfect jawline,
But he fell for her cute face,

She fell for his caring nature
But he fell for her carefree nature
She fell for his bossy nature
But he fell for her complaining nature
She fell for his present
But he fell for her past

She fell for his calmness
But he fell for her chaos
She fell for his classy behavior
But he fell for her homeless behavior
She fell for his smartness
But he fell for her goofiness

She fell for his silky hair,
But he fell for her untied hair
She fell for his cleanliness
But he fell for her mess

She fell for his looks
But he fell for her soul
He knew she was only attracted to him,
But still,
He was deeply in love with her

Dil Se Dil Tak

Kehena hain kuch,
Mere dil ko,
Tumhare dil se
Milna hain,
Meri nazron ko,
Tumhari nazron se

Aana jana hain mujhe,
Tumhare khayalo se,
Tumhare khayalo tak,
Manzil yehi hain meri,
Tumhare khwaabon se,
Tumhare khwaabon tak,

Kuch shikve mitaane hain,
Mere lafzon ko,
Tumhare lafzon se,
Milna hain,
Mere sapnon ko,
Tumhare sapnon se,
Aur,
Kuch baatein karni hain,
Meri baaton ko,
Tumhare baaton se,

Ab yehi hain,
Safar mera,
Mere dil se,
Tumhare dil tak ka!

They Are Perfect Together

He's eighteen, She's seventeen
He's mature, She's full filmy
He loves Hollywood, She loves Bollywood
He loves sun, She loves moon
He loves sunlight, She loves rains
He is her photographer, She is his model
He's fire, She's water
He likes coffee, She likes tea
He likes to listen to her, She likes to talk
She loves shopping,
He loves to carry her shopping bags,
She loves posing,
He likes to click her pictures
She loves to dance in rain,
He loves to watch her dance,
She likes listening to music,
He loves to sing for her,
He's her everything, she's all his
He's sunshine, she's raindrops,
And together,
They are a beautiful rainbow
Though they are opposite,
They have endless compassion for each other,
They have endless love for each other,
And that's why,
They are perfect together.

Mulaqaate

Hum roj milte,
Toh bohot logonse se,
Roj kafi logonse,
Takrate bhi hain,
Magar,
Kuch log aur unki mulaqaate,
Kuch khaashi hoti hain.

Woh mulaqaate,
Itni khaas hoti hain ki,
Humesha yaad banke,
Humare saath reheti hain,

Itni khaas hoti hain ki,
Un mulaqaaton ka,
Hum baar baar intezaar karte hain,

Itni khaas hoti hain ki,
Woh mulaqaate yaad karte hi,
Hum yuhi muskura baithte hain,

Aur
Itni khaas hoti hain ki,
Muskurate hi,
Woh pal aakhon ke saamne,
Firse aa hi jata hain

Kaash Unse,
Aankhe humari,
Baar baar milti
Aur,
Kaash woh mulaqaate,
Baar baar hoti,
Lekin kya kare?

Hum roj milte,
Toh bohot logonse se,
Magar,
Kuch log aur unki mulaqaate,
Kuch khaashi hoti hain.

Jab Hum Mile

Jab hum mile,
Pata nahi mujhe kya hua,
Peheli hi nazar mein,
Humne humara dil,
Aapke naam kar diya

Us din ke baad,
Zindagi aur haseen hogayi,
Us din Ke baad,
Zindagi aur geheri ho gayi
Zindagi mein mano,
Ek Jaadu sa hua,
Zindagi mano jaise,
Aur lambi hogayi,

Zindagi jine ke liye,
Aur ek bahana mil gaya,
Zindagi mein khush rehene ki,
Aur ek wajah mil gayi.
Zindagi ka ek naya,
Maksat jo mil gaya..

Is zindagi mein,
Bahot khush hain hum,
Is zindagi mein,
Bahot mashroof hain hum,
Aur,
Is zindagi mein,
Bahot kismatwale hain hum

Pehele bahot ghusail the,
Ab bade sharmile hain hum,
Pehele bahot nakchide the,
Ab bahot masoom hain hum,
Pehele paagal the,
Ab aur paagal hogaye hain,

Aap ke pyaar mein hum

Rehete ho tum,
Manjar mein hamare,
Baste ho tum,
Dil mein humare
Dilse tumhe,
Nikaal nahi paayenge,
Aur,
Tumhare bina,
Jee nahi paayenge hum..

Ishq Karke Bhi

Najdeek hoke bhi,
Najdeek na rahe hum,

Ek dusre ke saath hoke bhi,
Ek dusre ke na ho paaye hum,

Saath hoke bhi,
Khambhakat shikve dur na kar paaye hum

Aur,
Ishq karke bhi,
Unse ishq na kar paaye hum

Baarish

Mausam ye baarish ka,
Mausam ye khushiyon ka,
Mausam ye garajne ka,
Mausam ye barasne ka

Yeh baarish ka paani,
Rooh ko mere chhoohe,
Yeh baarish ka paani,

Yaad teri mujhe dilaye
Mohabbat barase
Meri zindagi mein,
Jaise Saawan mein
Baarish barase

Har pal mohabbat badhe
Jaise badhe baarish,
Mohobbat teri mujhe bhigaye,
Jaise bhigaye baarish

Bhigu mohabbat mein teri,
Jaise bhigu baarish mein,
Kho jau teri mohabbat mein,
Jaise kho jau baarish mein,
Yehi dua meine,
Ab mere rab se ki hain

Mausam ye baarish ka,
Mausam ye khushiyon ka,
Mausam ye garajne ka,

Mausam ye mohabbat barsane ka
Mausam ye leherane ka,
Mausam ye gungunane ka,
Mausam ye naachne ka,
Mausam ye nachane ka

Mausam ye ehsaas ka,
Mausam ye intezaar ka,
Mausam ye pyaar ka,
Mausam ye baarish ka

Our Bond Started To Fade

There was a time,
When I wanted to be with you,
There was a time,
When I carved for you,
There was a time,
When I loved you
And there was a time when,
Everything was alright,
Between me and you

There was a time,
When you were always there with me,
There was a time,
When you always wanted to see me smile,
There was a time,
When you always had time for me
And there was a time,
When you were all mine,

As the night changes,
Things between us too changed,
Everything became so strange,
It got so strained,
Just like our bond,
It started to fade

I started to loose my trust,
I started to feel locked,
I started to feel awkward,
But,
I never stopped loving you

There came a time,
When we drifted apart,
There came a time,
When everything became impossible,
And there came a time,
When everything was messed up

Still I didn't give up,
I chose to be with you,
I chose to wait for you,
I chose to keep loving you,
And,
I am still loving you

And that's my worst mistake!

Varsha Shailesh Bhosale (Ehsaas)

वर्षा एक उत्साही स्वनिर्मित व्यक्ति है। उसकी रुचि बहुत रचनात्मक कर्मो के साथ खेलते सीखते उभरती रही है। अनुभवों और भावनाओं को कागज़ पर व्यक्त करने की कला उसकी पहचान बन गई है। परिवार के लिए अपना समय व्यतीत कर संतुलन बनाए हुए कुछ समय खुद के लिए निवेश करती है, संगीत और कला के क्षेत्र में निपुणता की ओर अग्रेसर होते हुए। अपने जीवन में प्रत्यक्ष हुए अनुभवों, हृदय में उपजते अनेक भावनाओं और जग में विचरते हुए जो कुछ देखा, सीखा और ज्ञान प्राप्त हुआ उसी के आधार पर वर्षा ने कुछ कविताओं का संग्रह किया है। वर्षा ने 'गुलिस्ता -ए -जज़्बात ' नामक अपनी पहली पुस्तक भी एमेजॉन पर प्रकाशित की है।

कई बार मोहब्बत की है

तुझसे मैंने कई बार मोहब्बत की है,
तुझको चाहा, तुझको पूजा, तेरी बंदगी की है।

इस मोहब्बत ने हमें आज़माया हर क़दम पर,
बिछड़े मिलकर, फ़िर मिले कई बार बिछड़कर,
उस खुदा ने भी हमें कैसी तिश्नगी दी है।

है रौशन तू स्याह रातों में चांद की तरह,
बन जाऊं शिरीन मैं, इश्क़ तेरा फरहाद की तरह,
नाम तेरे मैंने अपनी ज़िंदगी की है।

तेरी दुनिया क्यों मेरी दुनिया से दूर नज़र आती है,
तेरे वादें, कसमें, वो इरादें, दिल को ना बहलाती है,
ये ना कहना तूने मुझसे दिल्लगी की है।

लौट आना जो जा चुके हो मुझसे दूर कहीं,
कोई भी राह चलो, देखो, मंज़िल तो है यहीं,
ये मोहब्बत ज़रा दीवानगी सी है।

तुझसे मैंने कई बार मोहब्बत की है।

जो कुछ तुझसे पाया है

तुझे ख़बर तो है ना, तू मुझमें ही समाया है,
खुशी हो, गम हो, आंसू हो, हंसी हो,
सब कुछ तुझसे ही तो पाया है।

याद है मुझे वो दिन जब ज़िंदगी ने मायूस कर दिया था,
तूने मेरे आंसुओं से भी मुस्कुराहट को ढूंढ लिया था।
दिल में थी मेरे कई बातें जो दर्द देती थी,
तूने बिन कहे भी मेरी ख़ामोशियों को पढ़ लिया था।
कहां वो समां था और कहां आज का ये मंज़र है,
ना वो तड़प मुलाक़ात की और ना अब हम मंज़ूर - ए - नज़र है।
है अब भी तुझे इश्क़ मुझसे कहीं लगता है मुझे,
पर कैसी ये बेरूख़ी, ये दूरी, ये क्या हो गया है तुझे।
ना देखना, ना मिलना, ना बात करना, ना पूछना हाल मेरा,
फ़िर भी क्यों बेचैन कर देता है मुझे हर पल खयाल तेरा।
आजा किसी दिन कह दे जो भी है तेरे मन में,
खुशियां पायी है तुझसे, खुशी ही चाहूंगी तेरे जीवन में।

हां, ये याद ज़रूर रखना, तू हर पल मुझमें ही समाया है,
इश्क़ है तू मेरा और मंज़ूर है मुझे जो कुछ तुझसे पाया है,
जो कुछ तुझसे पाया है।

जो गुज़ारी ना जा सके तुम बिन

जो गुज़ारी ना जा सके तुम बिन वो ज़िंदगी कैसी,
तुम रहो ना रहो साथ मेरे, दिल धड़कता तो रहेगा ही।

शिकायतें करूं आजमाइशों की मैं कितनी,
नेहमतों पर ही शुक्र जो मनाती मैं रही।

अपनों से खफ़ा होकर बैठूं, उन्हें संगदिल कहकर मैं क्यों,
गैरों के खुलूस से सुकूं पाती मैं रही।

इंतज़ार किसी हमसफ़र का क्यों करूं मोहब्बत की खातिर,
इश्क़ किया जब अपने वजूद से, ज़िंदगी मेरी निखरती रही।

अब ज़िंदगी ये गुज़ारनी नहीं है, साथ तुम्हारे या तुम बिन,
ज़िंदगी जीनी है अपने शर्तों पर, अब तक किसी ना किसी बंदिश में मैं रही।

जब मोहब्बत हुई

दिल में जैसे कोई हरारत हुई,
तुमसे मुझे जब मोहब्बत हुई।

नज़रें मिली, फ़िर झुकी, लब थरथराए, इक शरारत हुई,
तुमसे मुझे जब मोहब्बत हुई।

हर क़दम चलती जो पहले संभलकर, अब हर डगर पर है डगमगाती हुई,
तुमसे मुझे जब मोहब्बत हुई।

आंखें थी मेरी ख्वाबों से भरी, अब नींद है मेरी आंखों से ढलती हुई,
तुमसे मुझे जब मोहब्बत हुई।

चूमूं ये धरती छू लूं वो आसमां, हवाओं में फिरती हूं लहराती हुई,
तुमसे मुझे जब मोहब्बत हुई।

तुम संग सारा जहां लगता अपना सा, तुम बिन चांदनी रात भी है डराती हुई,
तुमसे मुझे जब मोहब्बत हुई।

साथ निभाऊंगी उम्रभर वादा रहा, साथ छूटेगा जब सांस होगी जाती हुई,
तुमसे मुझे जब मोहब्बत हुई।

ज़िंदगी का पहाड़

ज़िंदगी का पहाड़ सर करते जाना है,
लाख़ मुश्किल राह सही, सफ़र करते जाना है।

चलते जाते है हम शिखर तक पहुंचने को,
मंज़िल आने तक सफ़र से तजुर्बा पाना है,
ज़िंदगी का पहाड़ सर करते जाना है।

नदियां, गुंचे फूलों के और खुशगवार नज़ारें,
हंसी, खुशी और इत्मीनान के मोती चुनते जाना है,
ज़िंदगी का पहाड़ सर करते जाना है।

चलते हुए कई बार ठोकरें, ज़ख़्म भी शामिल हो जाते है,
दर्द – ओ – ग़म को मुस्कुराकर अपना हमराह बनाना है,
ज़िंदगी का पहाड़ सर करते जाना है।

इश्क़ किया नहीं जाता

इश्क़ किया नहीं जाता हो जाता है,
दिल दिया नहीं जाता को जाता है।

देखा जिसको हर रोज़ ख्वाबों ख्यालों में,
वो इक दिन बस यूंही सामने आ जाता है,
इश्क़ किया नहीं जाता हो जाता है।

बेचैनी होती है गर नाराज़ सनम हो जाएं तो,
मुस्कुराहट के लिए उसके, दिल तड़प जाता है,
इश्क़ किया नहीं जाता हो जाता है।

ज़िंदगी के हर मोड़ पर साथ चलने का वादा है,
पर कभी हमसफ़र मिलते मिलते बिछड़ जाता है,
इश्क़ किया नहीं जाता हो जाता है।

मैं फ़िर मिलूंगी

मैं फ़िर मिलूंगी तुझसे कभी,
वहीं मुस्कान होगी, वहीं प्यार होगा,
बस मंज़र अलग होगा।

मैं फ़िर मिलूंगी तुझसे कभी,
वहीं मुलाकातें होंगी, वही सिलसिला होगा,
बस मिलन का दायरा अलग होगा।

मैं फ़िर मिलूंगी तुझसे कभी,
दिल में तड़प होगी, इश्क़ बेशुमार होगा,
बस वो मक़ाम अलग होगा।

रात कहानी कहती है

रात कहानी कहती है जिसे सुन चांदनी सोती है।

इक मतवाली रात में चांद छाया बादलों पर,
कहता चांदनी से पास आ मेरे मुझसे ना डर।
चांदनी बस आसमां में यहां वहां टहलती है,
रात कहानी कहती है।

चांदनी लगे घबराई सी, फिरती है भरमाई सी,
चांद कहें आ संग मेरे, मुझसे क्यों शरमाई सी,
चांद की सुध ना चांदनी पलभर भी लेती है,
रात कहानी कहती है।

चांद कहें मैं रातों का राजा, दूंगा तुझे अभय आजा,
तेरे लिए सखा हूं नहीं राजा,अपने ग़म मेरे नाम लिखवा जा, चांदनी अब पहले
सी नहीं डरती है, चांद के संग सपने नए संजोती है।
रात कहानी कहती है।

चांद के बाहों में सिमटकर, रह गई चांदनी पिघलकर,
रोशन रात का तारा बनकर, चांदनी बिखरी दमककर,
प्यार में ये देखो इठलाती है, चांद के संग हाय इतराती है।
रात कहानी कहती है, चांदनी के संग खुश होती है।

ये इश्क़ हमारा तुम्हारा

तेरी इन बातों से मुझे शर्म आ रही है,
किस तरह कहूं आंखें तुम्हें देखें जा रही है,
होठों से लफ्ज़ कुछ कहने से थर्राते है
तू करीब हो तो मेरी ज़िंदगी हसीं होती जा रही है

तेरा नजदीकियां मेरे दिल को बहका रही है,
महक तेरी सांसों की मुझमें घुली जा रही है,
है लमज़ तेरे हाथों का अब तक मेरे हाथों पर,
ना जाने यह कौनसी घड़ी हमें पास ला रही है।

ए दिल नादानियां ना कर

ए दिल नादानियां ना कर,
तू रुसवा हो ख़ुद से ऐसी गुस्ताखियां ना कर।

ख़त्म होने को है आजमाइशें तेरी,
गम के अंधेरों में ख़ुद को ख्वार ना कर।

हुआ भी अगर तनहा तू अपनों की महफ़िल में,
गैरों के आगे अपनी बेबसी का इज़हार ना कर।

मौका परस्त है जहां सारा अपनी ही गर्ज़ की खातिर,
हर किसी की मोहब्बत पर एतबार ना कर।

तू ख़ुद है काबिल सिर उठाके जीने को इस माशरे में,
अपने लिए किसी सहारे की तलाश ना कर।

ए दिल तू नादानियां ना कर,
इश्क़ में किसी से आंखें चार ना कर,
फितरत है दिल तोड़ना हर आशिक़ की,
किसी रांझे से इस ज़माने के, हीर सा प्यार ना कर।

हर कदम साथ चलती है

एहसासों को ढांपने बड़ी सख़्त बन जाती है,
और कभी बस यूंही शबनम सी पिघलती है।

मुलाकातें ना हो तो रोज़ ख्वाबों में आ मिलती है,
उसके सिवा तारीफ़ कर दूं फूलों की तो
उन मासूमों से भी जलती है।

कहती है देखना चली जाऊंगी छोड़कर,
कैसे जान तुम्हारी मचलती है,
पर आ जायें जितने मुश्किल हालात सही,

हर क़दम साथ चलती है,
हर कदम साथ चलती है।

इल्ज़ाम

कहां उसने गुनाह मेरे या तो माफ़ कर दे,
या इल्जामों के साथ कोई सज़ा मुकर्रर कर दे।
सज़ा देना हम जैसे कमज़र्फ का काम कहा,
हम तो अपने ही सर कई इल्जाम लिए बैठे है।

Shalini Lakshman Rao

Shalini Lakshman Rao is a Brand and Communications Professional with over 30 years of experience in Advertising, Branding, Corporate Communications and Film Making.

Apart from being featured as a Poet of the month in Femina, her advertising work has also been featured in Lurzers, Archive.

She writes poems and fiction based on her observations of people and daily life.

She lives in Mumbai, India.

The Wait

The trees are shedding
Yellow leaves.
Autumn and high time
You looked at me.

Oedipus Rex

Mother, I want to curl up
In your womb
And not be born.

Mother, don't push me.

Suicide

The ground 24 floors below
Invites you to step off the ledge
See your whole life flash past
In fast-forward
As you discover
Yet another irony.

You want to live.

Calling Card

Whipped out of pockets
(At client meetings and networking seminars)
Shoved under table cloths
Left behind in loos
A collector's item
To be stored in files or boxes
Retrieved only when you want a favour.
It is light.
It is cumbersome.
It is an identity.

But most of the time, you just can't put a face to it.

The Lesson

Whenever grandpa farted
We were taught not to giggle
Or wrinkle our noses.
Just sit still for 30 seconds or so
And then, start breathing.

Awakening

My hands green and willowy
Reach out and touch the sky.
I always knew I existed.
Now I know the reason why.

Futility

Give me the vagrant meandering of your soul
The little secrets you store in recesses long forgotten
Long sighs of things that could be, or couldn't
And a look in the eye that
Makes promises you cannot keep.

En Route

Today, the 8.10 local from Badlapur
Solved the mystery of the unwhistling pressure cooker
Where in the knit there were two purls
And three dropped stitches.
Why the maid ran away with the watchman
And how the boss said 'good morning'
To the giggly bank clerk.
Missing the 8.10 is like missing your period.
Honeymoons are a bunch of photographs
With the husband's arm around the wife's shoulder
And nostalgia for other women.
Honeymoons are Ooty, Kashmir and Kodaikanal
Where the idea of a stranger making love to you
Is something to get used to because he is the husband.
Today the 8.10 had a panty seller
Who sold pink panties for Rs.30 a pair
And screamed that pink was a colour
Husbands liked as a rule but never said so.
Today the 8.10 had women with
Thinly threaded eyebrows
Unwashed hair
Purple lipsticks
Garlic breaths
Bushy underarms
And the kind of confidence
A Germaine Greer or a Gloria Steinem talks about.

Almost Thirty, Unmarried

Here I am on the threshold of thirty
An old maid to family, friends and acquaintances
Who've toed the line and produced children
For social respectability.

I've been spared the humiliation
Of being shown around coffee and conversation
That hinges around the books I've read
The music I listen to
While all the boy does is imagine me in bed
Virginal and ripe for his taking.

I've denied relatives the pleasure
Of complaining at my wedding about the food, the
presents and the groom's family.
I've puzzled matchmakers
By letting many a good catch
Slip out of my hands
Into the lap of a more willing bride.

Here I am on the threshold of thirty
Not entirely insensitive to a mother
Who prays that I discover
The joys of holy matrimony.

Priority

The flame that lit silences
Has burned out and left ashes
For tomorrow's prayer.
Treading on seeds Papa planted yesterday
I think of pursuits left behind
In pot joints and coffee shops

Touching wood, wearing amulets
Tying the black threads of Kashi around wrists
Why bathe in the Holy Ganga?
I'm afraid to be reborn a lizard.

In hushed whispers
I hear my father call.
Ma says the convent school may pollute my thoughts
And fill my head with Christianity.
It's a final threat.
The sun has scorched the cynic, my father
And scared him with damnation.

The habit fascinates me.
Blowing rings of smoke in toilets
Or letting Smack curl my hair
Till toes tickle.

Maybe I shouldn't have let that summer
Strip my defences and rape the grasses of thought.

Here I lie, thinking of Eliot and Pound
Willing to write and cannot
Because the sun set long ago
And the dark has filled me
With doubts I cannot clear.

Muzaina Tasneem

Muzaina exemplifies a well-rounded individual with a multifaceted approach to life. Her educational background in finance is demonstrably complemented by her operational expertise within the startup environment. Furthermore, her ongoing postgraduate studies reflect a commitment to intellectual growth and professional development. Beyond her professional pursuits, Muzaina fosters a deep appreciation for the finer things in life, finding solace in creative expression through poetry and cherishing the beauty of nature's simple wonders. Her affinity for animals is further evidenced by her attentive care for her feline companion, Cookie. Muzaina's knowledge of feline health and behavior makes her a valuable resource for those seeking guidance in pet care.

Symphony of Hues

With brush in hand, a whispered prayer,
A canvas bare, a world to share.
A symphony of hues I hold,
A story to be gently told.

The whites and blues, a summer sky,
A fiery red, where passions lie.
Emerald greens for whispering trees,
And ochres warm for autumn's breeze.

Each stroke a dance, a silent plea,
To capture light for all to see.
From sunlit fields to shadowed grace,
A world reborn in this small space.

The love of paint, a vibrant flame,
It ignites the soul, whispers my name.
A language spoken without sound,
A universe on hallowed ground.

In swirls and lines, emotions flow,
A joy unspoken, a quiet glow.
For in this art, my heart takes flight,
And paints the world in purest light.

Unleash the Whispers

A smothered fire within, an inner voice,
The heart has unlocked her deepest joys.
She wants to rise up, live in full public repute,
But the cloak of uncertainty stopping her pursuit.

Unveil your true colors - don't fear anyone,
Perpetual imagination be.
Take a brush, sing a false note
There is beauty in disorder, it is the world to make new.

Clear away the paints, and it will be done,
And forget about the masterpiece -let there be joy;
Write stories untold; dance in your kitchen
Let echo your laughter and never hold back on this
journey to freedom.

Seek magic amidst mundane leaves;
In cracking pavements, are tales that weave
Through skies' clouds and streams' gurgle,
And all these glimmers are sparks of creation.

Don't worry about judgment as you fail miserably;
Embrace flaws as they give birth to liberty
Creativity invites itself where the soul roams free,
Unfettered by constraints from an infinite decree.

So open that window and let sunlight through
Awake inner child let's win this duel with you.
Dare not go into unknown lands that lie around?
The space wherein your voice is found lies vast!

Unsilenced Melody

The melodies are humming in your heart,
The rhythms under your feet, eager to share
Don't let the music be silenced, the story your body tells,
In the power of dancing and singing, the magical world lives on.

The whispers of doubt may linger, a chorus of "what ifs,"
But passions are the embers that fan life's truest gifts.
Let your voice unfurl like a banner, bold and bright,
Let your body be the language, bathed in joyful light.

There will be interruptions and mistakes, a warning astray,
But with every practice your talent will find the way.
Turn off the negativity, the way is the means,
The fire within you, true beauty shines through.

So dare to take the stage, let your spirit soar,
Tell the hidden stories with music and light.
The world needs your creativity, a special dance for you,
Let your voice and body sing and take the throne you deserve.

For the passion for dance, the music that emerges,
The weaving of emotions, a story yet to be told.
So chase your dreams with enthusiasm, let your talents shine,
The world is waiting for your music, the dance of your heart and hands.

Threads of Passion

Let your heart sing with the click of needles,
Weaving stories in silken threads,
Paint with yarn, a world of textures,
Where dreams are unraveled and gently fed.

Like a sculptor shaping the formless clay,
Mold your passions, let your visions bloom,
Vases that hold whispers of a summer's day,
Cups cradling secrets to chase away gloom.

With each stitch, a whispered rhyme,
A tapestry rich with threads of time,
Let your spirit dance in the rhythm of craft,
A symphony born, a masterpiece laughed.

So pick up your needles, your threads so fine,
Let your soul take flight, a vibrant design,
For in the creation, your spirit takes hold,
A story unfolding, whispered, brave, and bold.

The Unscripted Stage

Let's sing a song of simple things,
The joys that everyday life brings.
Not grand parades or flashing lights,
But quiet pleasures, pure delights.

First, music's touch, a melody's grace,
A humming tune that fills the space.
A soulful strum, a rhythmic beat,
Tapping toes and hearts that meet.

Then, dance along, let worries fly,
With twirling skirts and reaching high.
No spotlight's glare, just pure release,
A joyful movement, bringing peace.

Crafting hands, with nimble art,
Transforming threads, a beating heart.
From yarn to scarf, from clay to vase,
Creation's joy, a warm embrace.

In fertile soil, a seed takes root,
Nurtured by care, a tender shoot.
Gardening's touch, a patient soul,
Watching life blossom, taking hold.

Words take flight, on wings of ink,
A tale unfolds, a mental link.
Writing's voice, a whispered rhyme,
A captured thought, across all time.

So find your joy, in big or small,
Let music play, and answer the call.
Dance with freedom, create with glee,
These simple treasures, set your spirit free.

The Whispering Star

A distant whisper, faint and far,
A guiding star, unseen, yet near.
Don't let the path seem long and stark,
Follow the dream, ignite the spark.

Though mountains rise, and shadows creep,
With steady steps, your journey keep.
For in the chase, the soul takes flight,
Embrace the challenge, chase the light.

For passions whisper, secrets told,
A map unfolds, a heart of gold.
In every stride, there's victory's call,
The whispering star will guide you all.

The Seed of Joy

A tiny seed, within you lies,
A dream's first breath, beneath the skies.
Don't let it wither in the shade,
Nurture the spark, with love pervade.

For passions bloom in fertile ground,
Where creativity can be found.
Let sunlight in, let worries cease,
Embrace the growth, and find your peace.

For joy takes root where dreams reside,
A blooming garden, deep inside.
With every leaf, a smile unfolds,
The heart contented, a story told.

Dance with the Wild

Don't tame the fire, let it roar,
The rhythm of your soul explore.
Embrace the wild, the untamed grace,
In every step, find your own space.

Let go of doubt, let freedom ring,
Where inspiration takes wing.
For passions sing a joyful tune,
A melody beneath the moon.

In swirling movements, light and free,
The truest version of you will be.
With every beat, your spirit thrives,
A dance of life, where passion survives.

Paint Your Sky

The world may offer muted hues,
But in your heart, a palette brews.
Don't shy from colors, bold and bright,
Paint your own sky, with all your might.

Let worries fade like morning mist,
Unfurl your flag, with dreams unkissed
By fear's cold touch. Take flight, take hold,
A story waits, in colors untold.

For passions sing a vibrant tune,
A melody beneath the moon.
In every brushstroke, find your bliss,
A masterpiece, a joyful kiss.

Unleash the Spark

A tiny ember, deep within,
A flicker of a dream unseen.
Don't smother it with doubt's cold hand,
Let passion's flame across you expand.

Think vast, beyond the narrow cage,
Where whispers turn the turning page.
Unleash the artist, wild and free,
Embrace the chaos, symphony.

For in the chase, the heart takes flight,
With every stroke, a starlit night.
The journey itself, a joyous song,
Where dreams ignite and spirits belong.

Shubham Sawant

Hi, I'm Shubham! Consider me as your friendly neighborhood poet, turning romantic moments, heartache, and unspoken feelings into poetry. As a part-time poet and full-time daydreamer, I love exploring the depths of the human heart, inspired by my 'fictional crush' and the world around us. You'll definitely find your own love story in my verses. My poems dive into themes of love, heartbreak, healing, self-reflection, inner turmoil, and reunion, all touching the core of human emotions. Reading them, you'll find a place to crash your emotions and maybe even heal a little.

Wish on the bed

Please let me live my life on my deathbed.

For once, I need to hear how my praises sound behind my back.

Where all the cherished memories went just for a sack.

For the sake of the love which I devoured for hatred.

Help me recouped the empty soul tethered.

Those will win over with a smile who play erroneous such is the sitch.

For all I still hope , there is a ray buoyant somewhere

Who changes the course of the firm, without sacrificing an humble soul

I'm tired now that my 7 minutes in life have been preached,

let me sleep with a dream to wake up in a place i wished.

Your Kind

I saw a herd going in and coming out
All walking the same steps

It was a big cage with closed window,
So as if the outer world was never an accessible source.

It amazed, fascinated, and mesmerized me to see the shine,
I went in, only to understand the ways of the dull corporate girnd.

I pledged to let me figure out my life, and one said the society is the dictator my child.
All had the same tongue, same mind, same kind, but all standing in a different line.

I ran from the cage, and got kicked back again by...,
The herd pushed me in, Crying to get out, but too pale to resist their force.

I heard them saying, why is this whine?
Only to realize, One day I have to become one of their kind.

Treasure Trove

I saw something in the deep pitch of the darkness.

It was my treasure trove of happiness,
I caught myself truly smiling.

I saw a dumb, a short, a fat, a thin, and a long
At that time we easily got well along

Then I saw my teachers,
a sweet, a stylish, a strict, and a sincere
All were following their perfect attitude even in here.

I saw a friend who deflected because of a small banter,
A single sorry from either side would've ended the matter.

I saw my first love, she wad still shining like a star,
I remember how I started blushing even at her sight from afar.

I closed the box in pain,
For everything just came to an end.

I tried to give my happiness one more life,
I went on forward without a cry

I thought of trying my luck in life one more time,
Whishing, nothing should've changed in a while.

I messaged everyone, "Hey old school friend",
To which a "Hi" is all they sent.

Know My Color

I wanted to exchange myself for the freight of food,
If only fuss could help me get it, I could.

My old ones are hungry, I swear,
Please show up god, if you really care.

I reflect on my order,
Like a miner craves for air.

I boarded the ship,
And hid myself in the deep

Suddenly a hand caught my rib,
A man appeared in the brim.

He investigated for my actions,
I promised to just have a packet of dim sums.

I was thrown at a superintendent's cell, and he yelled,
Who's this soil like creature you've held.

I was just offered a last wish to avail,
To which I replied, a place where racism does not prevail.

My Savior

Dreaming to meet you at the isle of ardour,
It has now become my proclivity.

Come save me for thee are my saviour,
Free me from my dolour.

I could notice you from afar,
As breeze carries your lushes
fragrance with sweet and sour.

There you come and could I see you.
You bowed down the society, the king, and the queen, and
love was that you withdrew.

I was mesmerized by the distance that grew,
If you'd looked closely you'd find someone dead in the
crew.

Old School Love

Maybe it was the fault of my old school love so far. that...

I drink your memories every night,
Just to take a glimpse of your sight.

Your walk, your talk, have pulled me out of my creative block.

The way you caressed your hair, Oh god!!
You killed me twice when you flipped your hair, I swear.

There's no law for this crime,
If were to make one, I'd say loving back your victim would be sublime.

I saw you smiling one night, and I was lost in your eyes at that sight.
My friends were the ones who helped me retract.

I read about the fairies,
With hazel eyes, delicate waist, and luscious hair.
OMG, they appear to be just like you.

They lied to me, that nymphs are only found in heaven,
Maybe they haven't seen you on this terrain.

I said, you should be among the wonders seven,
I showed your picture to make my claim even.

I relish my State, which is why,
I'm hiding my emotions in this cry.

I've put best time of my life in these lines,
Maybe you can hear them too if you try.

Surrender

I think, I should surrender to you...

Please let me surrender to you,
I'm tired of drowning in your feelings.

I write you, I think you, I crave you, I adorn you, i mourn
you, and what not. Should I go on?

My dreams are haunted by our memories to adorn,
I wish they could leave me alone.

I search for meaning in my poetry,
And your glimpse pass by quietly.

I've savoured the moments to the core,
which Every night I'm forced to adore.

I write your name in the my poems, that only you can
read,
On those memories every moment I feed.

And If you read them with the same feel,
There might be something between us still.

Coming Along

Breaking the shackles of the society,
We ran in the dark vehemently.
We asked them to let us live politely,
They read, the rules, the rituals, and the traditions out loudly.
Upon reaching the jungle's core,
We heard a quite noise at the shore.
We were in utmost shock,
Even here they've come to knock.
We ran even deeper in the jungle,
I wondered, could I even be the keeper of my word of honor!
There we met a north star,
He suggested to be firm on our place from afar.
They chased us and we became lifeless,
But we knew our paths were right, thanks to the stars grace.
We ran and fell and ran and fell,
and fell at last once and for all.
The sun, the moon, the starts gazing at us,
Tell them we're coming along.

Once And for All

I have to always beg you for the love,
Maybe that's how love is.
Or maybe there wasn't any!

Please put me out of this agony,
Loving, distancing, distressing, hurting,
This wasn't supposed to be this way.

I remembered our first talk, first walk and first eye lock.
All was pretty, but now it's as dreadful.

Was it always the same? Or was I blinded by love?

Eyes could be fooled, but how can gut be wrong?
What's the reason that our relationship couldn't hold
strong?

The days haunt me when I was in a plight,
Your help could've consoled me, but you always lied.

I saw you change in front of my eyes, it was your call.
If only it was this easy to end all.

No where it's written that one should suffer under one's
shawl.
That's when I decided it's time to move on, once and for
all.

Introvert's Love Story

By the tree I sat, with all my memories intact.
The flower, detached to rest on my hand which felt like an attack.

I shouted, please don't do this,
I'm lost in something spectacular.
The look that it gave me was extremely peculiar.

I acted to be vain, You can't get your thoughts out of me.
I act weird in front of you and always make a fool of me.

Your presence is the most I crave,
But it's the same thing that hold me from being brave.

A lot is going on in my head,
If you shake me, I bet my words would shed.

Ahh, so you're still in the shell,
What is it that's stopping you to tell.

Asked the tree when I was on the move,
Tell me, tell me, written on the leaf that fell on my shoe.

Tell me Why was that fright,
because It was an introverts love story I cried.

Ocean Inside Me

You know there's this thing with the poets,
They love to exaggerate everything...

Or maybe it's how they love!!!

I remember you talking, and me nodding,
You smiling and me melting.

I was too obvious,
But you too careless to notice.

I can sacrifice the sight of the sun, the moon, and the stars
It's the matter of a moment with you, Afterall.

You said your poetry inspiration is unreal.
Maybe, you haven't come across yourself.

I'm yet to find after sun, moon, and warmth of an igloo,
Someone as beautiful as you.

The gaze, when I Look at you, then look away when I get caught, yes that awkward moment.
I don't wanna show,
I'm shy but i still want you to look at me.
I want you know my heart beats your name and craves your presence.

I will say each and every thing from rain to flowers and stars to describe you,
but dare come to the point.

I'm dancing while writing,
there's rejoice and turmoil inside me.

I'm just expressing the surface,
Please read the ocean inside me.

Kaleidoscope of Our Memories

Do you know what I see from the toy I'm holding,
Let me tell you!

I see us, when we were children,
Young, happy, and joyful.

Hey, I could see us laugh,
remember when we used to catch the shaft?

I could see us quarreling over those pancakes,
When you upset you put everything at stake.

Let me turn the wheel.
Ohh! We are little grown up now.

I could see you doing well in your hobbies, and actions
Alas, We've found our passions.

You won the writing Competition,
I see you happy planning our next vacation.

Turned the wheel,
Ohh! We are teens now.

I see us struggle with our body notions,
Omg, we fight to control our emotions.

I could see us all over the place, constant fights, stolen
glance, and ego upright,
I could see us greying our life in front of my sight.

A little more turn to the wheel, why's it grey?
There's something wrong with the scope it's lost colour.
Ohh! Here we're as Adults!

I see us behaving like kids,

Constant fights, lost life, and broken hearts, to say the least.

I see us, both on our own way,
Hurts to see us drifting away.

A last turn, the kaleidoscope broke!!
What do we do now?

I want to make it colorful again,
But how?

Let's try to be kids again!
Who's joy never went to vain.

Hold your kaleidoscope and check thou,
Is everything all right and colorful now?

Swapnadip Bhattacharya

Swapnadip Bhattacharya is an emerging poet whose evocative verses explore themes of nature, identity, emotions and the complex psyche of humans. His captivating work draws readers in with its vivid imagery and emotional depth. He is a literature enthusiast who still embraces the old-school poetry of verses and rhymes contrasting the modern poetry. He looks for an emotional touch in a bland, competitive, and cold world.

Feel free to drop your comments or suggestions at- swapnadipbhattacharya7@gmail.com

A Night's Lament

A deserted avenue, so long,
Thirsty for footsteps, evening crowd's cheer,
Silent streets where echoes throng,
Lonely nights are drawing near.

A dark, black sky, so still,
Clouds veil the midnight's shine,
Branches bare on the hill,
Void of songs once so divine.

A forest of concrete, tall,
Reaching high, no life in sight,
A lamppost stands, a glowing call,
In the depths of silent night.

A distant tower's red light,
Flashes in the quiet air,
The breeze flows with gentle might,
Silence screams, an empty prayer.

A frame of flesh, without a spark,
Leans on a parting, old and frail,
Eyes gaze at the face, now dark,
Tears fall for love's last tale.

A Beat Away

Till the love departs, someday soon,
On a deserted roof or a crowded mall,
We face the quiet, beneath the moon,
Our hearts in silence, rise and fall.

Till our eyes meet, by chance or fate,
You lay besides, or pass the door,
In moments shared, we hesitate,
A glance that speaks, forevermore.

Till our skins touch, in truth or lie,
In clouded sheets or through our tears,
We seek the warmth, the reasons why,
In whispers soft, our deepest fears.

Till hearts do beat, in sync or stray,
Breath heavy, lips stitched tight,
Through love or loss, come what may,
In shadows dark, or morning light.

Till love's wild vice, untamed and free,
Falls upon the setting day,
Bound together, you and me,
Just a beat, a breath away.

Whispers on the Sand

By the waves on wed sand,
I lie stark naked, body and soul,
Waiting for your gentle hand,
To soothe my heart and make me whole.

Till you come through tempest's might,
To touch my soul and wake my heart,
Guiding me from endless night,
To where our lives no more depart.

The waves will carry us afar,
To a world where we belong,
Beneath the same eternal star,
In a place of love so strong.

Till then I wait upon this shore,
In slumber deep, my heart confined,
Dreaming of our love once more,
Your eternal presence in my mind.

Till the storm's wild fury fades,
And you sail to find my side,
We'll journey through the sunlit glades,
Where dreams and love abide.

In a Misty Serenity

A thousand years later, in the alley's gloom,
Of my memories, where sands stretch wide,
Will you still plague my mind with bloom,
And plant a seed where tears abide?

In the barren cracks of my solitude,
Your love once vibrant, now a haunting trace,
Will it sprout again in quietude,
In shadows where my sorrows race?

The memories with you, now distant, cold,
A mist clouds my mind, emotions fade,
Your thoughts haunt my soul, fires bold,
In desire's flames, my heart is laid.

My eyes, flooded with tears unshed,
Held back by a promise, deep and true,
To someone in serenity's stead,
In misty calm where dreams renew.

Will you linger in the twilight's fold,
As time weaves tales of what we've lost,
In echoes of our love retold,
Through the years and countless cost?

A thousand miles and sands of time,
Cannot erase the pain we feel,
Your presence still a haunting rhyme,
A wound that time can never heal.

In dreams, I see your fleeting face,
A ghostly vision, bittersweet,
In the depths of this endless space,
Where memories and heartbeats meet.

My eyes, flooded with tears unshed,
Held back by a promise, deep and true,
To someone in a misty serenity,
Where I forever wait for you.

Denied by Death

My blood-red eyes in quest of peace,
Came across the solitary death,
At the country crossroads' eerie cease,
Where silent shadows hold their breath.

My stitched lips spoke in silent plea,
To join him for eternal rest,
But death denied, spoke life to me,
And virtues countless he professed.

My numb and tired brain then thought,
Was he even speaking true?
"No, he's not," my mind distraught,
Yet the urge to join him grew.

My boiling skin then froze in place,
My clouded sheath spat crimson flood,
Cried for icy hell's embrace,
As dawn broke with its golden blood.

Death then spoke in solemn tone,
"I cannot take you yet, my friend,
For time still left, you'll walk alone,
Till fate decrees your end.

Till then, endure the living lie,
The sins you cause will pile high,
And only then, beneath the sky,
Shall you be allowed to die."

Lost Days of Youth

Walking down the street one day,
I saw a little boy so small,
He didn't have food to eat or play,
Nor a toy to call his own at all.

I thought deeply and realized then,
It's not just one child in despair,
Thousands suffer this fate, where men
Have stolen childhood's joy to wear.

Food and clothing, their only need,
They toil to make ends meet,
Guilt weighs heavy, a bitter seed,
Shame to humanity's defeat.

I too once shared their plight,
A childhood lost, under open skies,
Worked all day and into the night,
For mere scraps and meager lies.

Childhood now fades swiftly away,
As everyone strives to be the best,
No moment wasted, no time to play,
Hearts and minds denied their rest.

One day, all that's sought and claimed,
Money, fame, mansions tall,
Yet childhood, lost and unnamed,
Can never be regained at all.

Let's cherish the innocence gone,
Restore the laughter, joy, and mirth,
For every child, a brighter dawn,
Where dreams flourish, and hearts find worth.

A Silent Cry

A grave they laid before my eyes,
Your image fading with each passing day,
Even after my futile cries,
You've departed, no longer to stay.

My dear friend, for countless days,
Side by side we walked this earth,
Now it's time for you to part ways,
Leaving behind aching dearth.

I gather what I can of you,
Your belongings now in my care,
Yet frozen before me, you lay true,
I can't endure this grievous stare.

I hold onto your priceless memories,
But this harsh world proves them wrong,
I recall your words, your theories,
Now silenced by death's final song.

I told you once, you'd not forget,
A bird can't soar without its feather,
You sought to fly, with no regret,
Now finding peace beneath the heather.

No one's left for you or me,
We were each others guiding light,
Yet you departed alone, you see,
Leaving your brother to fight.

Oh, how I mourn your loss, dear friend,
In this world now so bleak and cold,
Our bond, now broken, cannot mend,
As I hold onto memories, precious as gold.

Rest now, in eternal peace,
Far from this world's pain and woe,
In the realm where sorrows cease,
May your spirit forever glow.

Whispers of Dawn

I lay still on dew-kissed grass,
Gazing at the misty sky,
Morning's cold caress does pass,
Soft whispers as time slips by.

Suddenly, I pondered deep,
What if fate had been unkind?
What if I could not see or peep,
Cursed, blind, in darkness confined?

Would these misty mornings hold,
Such love and tender grace?
Or snowy mountains, tales untold,
Their curves in gentle embrace?

How would the summer sun's bright glow,
Dance upon my eager eyes?
Raindrops falling soft and slow,
Would miss my gaze in somber skies.

I know the rain would still descend,
From heavens far and high,
Yet I'd not see how they wend,
Through darkness where shadows lie.

My days would be but gloomy plight,
Nights draped in endless dark,
Each step a weary, lonely fight,
No beauty to ignite a spark.

I'd miss your beauty, oh so fair,
And thrilling moments shared,
I'd sit alone in deep despair,
Unseen, unloved, and unpaired.

I'd curse the heavens, bitter and sore,
For every breath I took,
Life's limits darkened to the core,
In shadows where dreams forsook.

But thank the stars it is not so,
For light and sight are mine,
Every sight, every touch, bestow,
Beauty's kiss, so divine.

Grateful now for every sight,
Every sound, every touch,
In this world so wondrous, bright,
Love's embrace, I cherish much.

A Tale of two Sunset

The sun sank low with measured tread,
As I walked the road in haste,
Escaping missteps that I dread,
In the evening's tranquil embrace.

Upon a rag, a small boy slept,
Beside him, a bowl and toy,
In dreams where innocence is kept,
Unaware of the world's coy.

The bridge stood silent in the dusk,
Save for stray dogs' playful dance,
And shadows flit, shadows dusk,
In the fleeting twilight's trance.

His innocent face held my gaze,
I forgot my troubles and flight,
Lost in his peaceful, quiet ways,
A fleeting respite from the night.

I approached with silent care,
He slumbered, untouched by plight,
No possessions, no burdens to bear,
In the calm of fading light.

A weight bore down on my soul,
How selfish my path had been,
Where had my restless footsteps strolled,
In search of solace unseen?

Sirens echoed down the avenue,
In the deserted evening's shade,
Yet I stood there, seeking anew,
A path where peace could be laid.

Twelve years on, I returned once more,
To that quiet, forsaken lane,
The sun set, the sky aglow with lore,
In colors of twilight's reign.

The boy still slept, unchanged in rest,
Time's touch had left him serene,
But I, bidding life a final quest,
Found solace in the tranquil scene.

Whispers on the Tide

On a fine winter morning's grace,
I strolled along the quiet road,
Dew kissed the grass in soft embrace,
Above, the sun in splendor glowed.

The trees whispered with a lustful sway,
Birds conversed in branches high,
Fishermen lads in haste made way,
Their silhouettes against the sky.

Ocean waters kissed the sand,
Erasing steps once boldly taken,
Shoreline washed by gentle hand,
With grains of sand their burden shaken.

The beach embraced the rolling tide,
Rising, breaking with rhythmic zest,
And boats afar, serene they glide,
On waters where they find their rest.

The sun, now gleaming bright and clear,
Mist of dawn now fades from view,
Its red hue whispers of the year,
Awakening skies in morning's brew.

Along the shore, I wandered free,
Footprints left behind with care,
A man walked, eyes seeking sea,
His face a mask of quiet prayer.

He sought answers in the breeze,
Questions lingered, yet unknown,
Canvas of waves, a whispering tease,
In their ebb and flow, life's monotone.

Searching for a part undone,
In life's tapestry, scorched and tried,
Yet amid trials, battles won,
Begins anew the winsome stride.

A Tiny Traveler

On a coat of silky silk,
As buttery, creamy milk,
A black, tiny, lonely ant,
Walking slowly, adamant.

I was sitting on a chair,
Under the lamp's bright glare,
Sudden I saw the tiny black,
On my cupboard's second rack.

With a tiny bit of food,
Adorned in yellow hood,
He marched on a silent quest,
Driven by some unseen zest.

Tiny steps on paths uncharted,
Through a world so vast and guarded,
His journey seemed so small and frail,
Yet his spirit did not pale.

As he ventured, undeterred,
Life's fragility inferred,
In his persistence, lessons drawn,
From dusk till the breaking dawn.

The next day, once more he came,
Bearing yellow hood the same,
Started from my room again,
Winding through the morning rain.

Onward to a world unknown,
In his solitude alone,
Yet the journey he'd begun,
Vanished ere the day was done.

In his trek, a metaphor,
For life's fleeting, fragile core,
But alas, his journey ceased,
In the shadows, life released.

With his tiny form now still,
In the quiet, my heart did fill,
With thoughts of life's tender span,
Ephemeral, like the ant's brief plan.

In his end, a silent plea,
For fragile life and harmony,
In his tiny world, he showed,
Life's delicate, gentle ode.

For I have Sinned

In twilight's glow first, I saw her grace,
A crimson light upon her face.
My heart was hers from that first sight,
My queen, my love, my guiding light.

Each day I'd walk and see her there,
A vision pure beyond compare.
One eve she vanished, lost from sight,
I searched and searched, consumed by endless night.

Into a darkened lane I strode,
A call, a scream, then cries that slowed.
I ran to where the shadows played,
Four devils there, a girl betrayed.

I fought, but three of them had fled,
The fourth struck down her weary head.
I hurled at them, tried to save,
Too late, she lay within her grave.

Her eyes, once bright, now void of light,
Her blood and tears a dreadful sight.
I held her close, my soul in pain,
A love now lost, a heart in chain.

My chest gave out, I fell beside,
Awoke to guilt I could not hide.
Her parents' cries, the judgment made,
The world believed the lies conveyed.

Freed by the law, yet bound by shame,
Her memory burns deep like a flame.
I long for peace, to end the fight,
To join her serenity in the endless night.

In twilight's shadow, demons danced,
Their cruel hands upon her chanced.
Her cries now haunt my every breath,
A symphony of pain and death.

I see her face in dreams so stark,
A bleeding angel in the dark.
Her purity, now stained and torn,
A rose amid the cruelest thorn.

I live in Hades, shadows' curse,
In agony, this endless verse.
Medusa's gaze, the world's disdain,
Eternal night, perpetual pain.

So now I leap, the water calls,
The air, the plunge, as darkness falls.
I seek her where the silence lies,
To prove my love and say goodbyes.

For I have sinned by loving true,
By failing her, by all I do.
Her blood, my tears, a testament,
In death, perhaps my soul finds rest.

So let me fall, to Lethe's stream,
Forget my sin, dissolve my dream.
To meet her where the angel's dwell,
And break this sorrow's mortal spell.

For in my heart, her whispers stay,
A ghost that never fades away.
Her blood, my tears, forever bind,
In death, perhaps, peace I will find.

Manasi Manchanda

I don't just wish to be a writer but do something beyond with my art...
To move across your mind, find a place to reside in your heart...
I don't just write to tell my story and my experiences being revealed...
For I write with a hope to touch your wounded heart and an earnest desire to heal
-Manasi M.
Manasi Manchanda, a psychology major, is an innocent, zealous and humble girl.
Driven by her innate passion of psychology, she had pursued several short-term certifications in the field of psychology such as criminal/forensic, children to geriatric psychology etc. just to name a few.
She is also a trained pistol shooter for India up to national level.
She is also the girl behind the full stop to semicolon community born after having authored the book 'Journey full stop to semicolon' as an international author published with Olympia Publishers, UK, available worldwide.
But most importantly she is girl just like you, strongly determined by her own experiences of clinical depression, autoimmune disorder and such hardships, resolute and driven to unveil self-attainable happiness and turning full stops into semicolon.
To discover more of my words and get in touch...
Find me on...
Instagram- @journey_fullstop_to_semicolon
E-mail- manasi2602@hotmail.com

Explaining My Depression

Explaining my depression was downright the most difficult
task I had to do...
As transitory sadness, lack of friends and escapism it was
repeatedly misconstrued.

Anxiety ruthlessly held me a hostage inside of my house,
inside of my bed...
Insomnia swept me in its arms each night while I battled
the voices inside my head.

I don't want your good advice to divert my mind or
reasons why I'm alright...
My smile just a reflection of politeness while inside me a
constant battle I fight.

And all those nights you told me to leave my laptop, get
more sleep, give my mind some rest...
Oh, how I wish I could sleep, but I was busy avoiding
confronting the empty side of my bed.

Don't tell me that I'm making something out of nothing
and that I'm better than this...
For depression wasn't a choice I made but a disease in the
form of a curse that had held me by the wrist.

You ask me if I'm lonely and you think I'm lying when I
tell you I'm not alone...
For depression is like an uninvited roommate living with
me even before I had ever known.

Humans ought to make mistakes mom said, so for all your
judgments today I'm forgiving...
How conveniently you think that I'm afraid of dying, but
trust me in this world I'm afraid of living.

All Or Nothing at All

I could be your all or nothing at all...
A good morning kiss or just a late-night call.

The one you hugged tight to sleep or just a bedtime thought...
I could be your bride, or the affair with which you get caught.

The one you cook for on date nights, or to whom you get casual flowers sent...
the one to whom you make love with passion, or just a meaningless sexual vent.

The one who carries your baby within, or the one whose dirty tales you told...
An immortal love, whose story you just can't wait to tell or just a casual fling even whose mention you withhold.

I could be you biggest achievement or your gravest fall...
I could be your all or nothing at all.

Refused to Fight

Disillusioned with happiness at such tender age
The anguish and adversity in words I just can't phrase
The air around me still feels like a cage
As a million ruthless voices within me rage

Been struggling and fighting for as long as I know
My innocence snatched, forced to grow
My smile was taken long ago
It took the death of hope to let it go

Spit your pity against the stones
And place yourself against my soul
Sleeping at nights with a heart that moans
Oblivious, if it will ever again be whole

The agony and despondency is beyond what I can show
My faith and hope was banished long ago
What future holds and all my dreams away I throw
If you love me let me go, run away before we know

In this brutal fight each day a part of me dies
Breathing each day, but am I really alive?
I couldn't come this far without your hopeful lies
But all of that was ripped apart when my heart refused to fight

Sacred Relationship

My partner in crime and a constant dependable listener to fall back on
A different kind of sacred relationship, a friend with a tail and 4 tiny paws

Helpless, debilitated we stood aghast in front of decisions of time
When suddenly you refused to play any longer, your paws slipped away from mine

I would give up the world just to hold you in my arms once again
But I choose to let you go to sleep than suffer with the excruciating and undeserved pain

You were my home, my hope and your mischievous ways the reasons for my smile
So no, I won't shed anymore tears but cherishing the happy memories forever keep you alive

Detached

In the dark I stand alone,
Away from comfort, away from home...

Distanced from love and warmth around,
Succumb to weakness I fall to ground...

Emotions severed I feel so numb,
To this isolation, I succumb...

Expectations remain forever unmatched,
But now I'm broken, exhausted and detached...

The struggles and defeat is unimagined,
In this forever lost battle, you just can't fathom...

The adversity, pain and affliction around,
Succumb to weakness I fall to ground...

To make a difference is all I wish I could,
As I stand alone forever misunderstood...

Of all the fortitude I had been snatched,
I'm broken, exhausted and detached...

I hope the wounds someday would heal,
Reducing the distress today I feel...

All the lessons learnt to retain in mind,
I wish the scars to stay behind.

My Struggles You Will Never Know

Innumerable hope ignited within,
To prove to the society, I had to show...
Trying to exceed my capabilities each time,
My struggles you will never know.

All the wishes and things I put aside,
How much I wish if I could just borrow...
Few minutes without having to prioritize,
My struggles you will never know.

Distanced from friends and things I love,
Those carefree laughs behind I throw...
Always under the pressure of the future,
My struggles you will never know.

Devoid of a peaceful night's sleep,
Surrounded by misery, dejection and sorrow...
The battle I fight inside my head each day,
My struggle you will never know.

Caught in the rut of expectations,
Trying so hard to go with the flow...
Not giving into these arduous circumstances,
My struggles you will never know.

All those nights devoid of sleep,
And all the tears I cried alone...
Unaided this phase I ought to fight,
My struggles you will never know.

Hoping To Be Proven Wrong

Broken, fragmented by the past,
Strong-headed, independent she knew...
Skepticism about everything would forever last,
Experiences of life had destroyed her views.

Unwilling to lay her trust on another,
She wanted to remain detached, distanced and aloof...
Getting closer meant risking her heart, already so heavy,
Carrying innumerable scars from past as a proof.

With a soul so heartbreakingly fragile,
Had been raging through storms alone for long...
An inexplicably beautiful paradox she had become,
With a heart and mind unbreakably strong.

Reasons behind her dissociation and silence,
Are not that she had nothing in mind...
So much so tightly packed with emotions,
Where to start as impossible to find.

With all these feelings inside her head,
Silently in a pool of sorrow she soaked...
Her heart so heavy, her head so sore,
Being awaken to reality her strength just broke.

Happiness, love, forever's are just an illusion,
She had developed such views so unshakably strong...
Yet deep inside her heart within,
For once she was hoping to be proven wrong.

When Friendships Change

In our hearts at young age, the seeds of friendship are sown...
Taught to love, care and be honest, and never to leave them alone.

To do the thing that is right, is what a friend must advise...
Through the adversaries, pain or tough times, a friend is one who can help you rise.

A friend is someone who can breakdown, a wall that you have built...
And go beyond the fake smiles on your lips, to reach the heart, with pain that's filled.

Friends, they say are like siblings, that God forgot to give...
They promise to be there by your side, for all the years you live.

Yet driven by materialistic desires, and forgetting the promises made at the start...
Over the times, things just changed, and friendships fall apart.

Yet the memories and times spent, can't just cease to matter...
Though the dependence faith and trust, without a care they shatter.

Not a quitter or escapist, it's only after several tries that I decide...
To keep the pain deep inside and next time, my heart, I'd rather hide.

When I Run

The painful, still recent scars I had learnt to flaunt,
Yet the memories intact continued to haunt...
As flashbacks when I was asleep or awake,
Into a shudder of fear my soul would break.

Tough on the outside "oh she's now all fine" they said,
As I failed to express how those days I just couldn't
forget...
Carrying on with life, keeping those days aside,
The post traumatic pain, now I had mastered to hide.

Ask me if I'm still haunted by those memories,
And I would have poured my heart out to extremities...
But these feelings and thoughts I instead dismissed,
Only to find ignorance isn't always bliss .

So when I run and work for long,
It isn't ego, pride or just being headstrong...
I run from being strong and always pretending to be fine,
And the pain that within these walls of strength each day
remains confined.

And no its not another sob story of lost hope,
Contrarily my individualized ways to cope...
I run not to be appreciated that I'm brave or told I'm
wrong,
I just run to remind myself what it feels like to be strong.

If I Don't Come Home

On all those cold, exhausting worked up nights,
I put the blanket on and hug you tight...
So if someday I'm knocked down, and I don't come home,
Forgive my misery and promise to triumph this journey on your own...
Let go of the grief, take a deep breath and turn off the lights,
For I'll be right next to you, my soul hugging you tight.

When your hunger is outweighed by work and time,
How adorably you loved being fed by hands, but only mine...
So if someday I'm knocked down, and I don't come home,
Forgive my misery and promise to triumph this journey on your own...
You'd say agony of loss has seized your hunger for life,
But remember each time I cooked for you and seeing you eat how I smiled.

The enthusiasm that drove us to each coffee shop we won't let die,
Making coffees so perfect as I mix sugar in yours and you mix it in mine...
So if someday I'm knocked down, and I don't come home,
Forgive my misery and promise to triumph this journey on your own...
Don't let our memories barricade the coffee stories you lived each time,
Fearless you go to our same cafes, but I hope you think of me once in a while.

A room full of babies, we gifted each other every once in a while,
Whether mickey, Minnie or teddu, always loving and pampering them alike...
So if someday I'm knocked down, and I don't come home,

Forgive my misery and promise to triumph this journey on your own...
When I'm not around, and you feel alone on cold silent nights,
Feel my smile in your memories, kiss on your forehead as you hug them tight.

On all the road trips we escaped reality just hugging each other tight,
As I rest on your shoulders with loud music, us singing, and our silly little fights...
So if someday I'm knocked down, and I don't come home,
Forgive my misery and promise to triumph this journey on your own...
Don't just escape the city to forget the memories as endlessly alone you drive,
I hope you remember the songs I sang for you and as you drive they make you smile.

Mundane Days

And one day you will find yourself pinning for the most mundane days with me...
All those little moments within the routine that mattered the most but you couldn't see.

All those moments we missed as I waited, while you entangled in work, just work that surround...
One day you'd realize why I urged over the mundane routine, but I would no longer be around.

You'd silent your phone, shut your laptop and come running looking for me...
For that is the day you'd find yourself pinning for the most mundane days with me.

I don't know if, up in the sky among the stars, or buried deep within the ground...
One day when you come running looking for me, I would no longer be around.

Somedays

Some days I still miss the way you hugged me tight...
Some days, I miss our sleepy talks on the cold and
lonesome nights.

Some days I can't help wonder if you would have found
someone new...
Some days I can't help wonder do you think of me
sometimes too?

Some days I wish to lean on your chest a bit longer for one
last time...
Some days I miss walking around holding your arms, like
you are just mine.

Some days I wish my phone to read your name when it
rings for someone calling...
Some days I miss how you pulled me in and held me tight
just to prevent me from falling.

Some days I miss your kiss on my lips, but the one on my
forehead a little more...
Some days I miss our silly little fights that we resolved with
cute ways to say sorry and never keeping scores.

Some days I miss the way you called my name but more
the way you said you loved me the most...
No doubt we shared the most significant ups and downs,
but all the happiness came with a cost.

Some days I miss how you looked me in the eyes with
passion, as if to never blink them away...
An atheist, I don't believe in God but to bring back those
days some nights I silently pray.

Anlet Nevi J

With a rich background in software engineering spanning over a decade, I am a skilled professional who thrives on solving complex challenges in the realm of technology. Raised amidst Kerala's vibrant landscapes, I have mastered the intricacies of codes and algorithms, bringing creativity and finesse to every project.

However, beyond my technical expertise lies the heart of a dreamer who has always harbored a deep passion for writing. Life's path led me into engineering, where I honed my skills and excelled, yet the ember of writing continued to burn brightly within me.

Now, I am reigniting my love for writing, embracing poetry as a new creative outlet. I am navigating this journey with enthusiasm, pouring my soul into words to capture emotions, stories, and experiences.

Symphony of Tangled Fires

In shadows deep, my heart does dwell,
Between two loves, a tangled plight,
One gentle touch, a soothing spell,
The other, passion's fierce delight.

They say one cannot love two more,
Yet here I stand, my soul in strife,
For how to choose, what to adore,
When each brings color to my life?

Her laughter, like a summer's day,
Warm and bright, a tender grace,
The other's fire, a wild array,
A tempest I can't help but chase.

No scale can measure love's embrace,
Nor weigh the worth of hearts' desires,
Two different songs, one heart, one voice,
A symphony of tangled fires.

Tresses of Elysium

A strand of midnight, soft and fine,
I hold it close, in secret grasp,
Yearning for the day you'll learn,
How my heart beats at your command.

Your hair, a cascade, dark and deep,
I wonder at its silken flow,
Imagining the secrets it keeps,
The scent that lingers, soft and slow.

Would it feel like gentle rain,
Or velvet whispers, soft and warm?
To lose myself in its refrain,
And shelter from the world's alarm.

Oh, tresses of Elysium,
In you, a universe unfurled,
Each strand a thread of pandemonium,
In this silent dance, love swirled.

But until the moment I confess,
This hidden longing, sweet and true,
Your hair, my only tenderness,
Binds me close, in thoughts of you.

Sip of Redemption

Bitter brew, once a relentless foe,
In the morning haze of toil and woe,
Each cup a weight, heavy to raise,
As a waitress in the dim-lit maze.

The aroma clung, a haunting veil,
Of battles fought, stories frail,
Coffee stains marked her sleeve,
Remnants of struggles, hard to believe.

But today, a shift, a subtle turn,
She raises the cup, no longer spurned,
A sip, tentative, taste hesitant,
Flavors awaken, not a moment spent.

Bitterness now a subtle charm,
Resilience echoes, once disarmed,
In each sip, a grace newfound,
A journey's triumph, peace unbound.

Song in the Empty Room

In days gone by, he asked for just one thing,
A melody to soothe, a voice to sing,
Yet time slipped through, with tasks to tame,
And her song remained a whispered name.

Now, in quiet hours, memories cascade,
Echoes of his smile, his love portrayed,
Each note she could have sung, now clear and strong,
Yet he's beyond the reach of her heartfelt song.

Regrets play softly, like a gentle breeze,
As she recalls his faith in melodies,
In dreams deferred, she finds a solemn grace,
In the space where his presence used to trace.

If only time rewound, and she could share,
The song he longed for, in the evening air,
But today, she sings into the empty room,
Her voice a tribute in the silent gloom.

A Taste of Love

In the kitchen's gentle hum, he stands,
Crafting flavors with tender hands,
Each ingredient a love untold,
In pots and pans, their story unfold.

The aroma, like a whispered vow,
Fills the room, serenades her now,
Her smile, a taste of joy and grace,
Reflects his heart in every embrace.

The sizzle of spices, a delicate dance,
Echoes of their shared romance,
As he seasons with passion and care,
Her happiness, his culinary prayer.

Around the table, candles aglow,
They sip and savor, aflow,
For in each bite, in every taste,
Their love resounds, never to waste.

In his cooking, their bond so clear,
A feast of love, year after year,
With every dish, his love he sends,
A taste of forever, beyond all ends.

The Eternal Torment

Oh, Desire, with your beguiling art,
You grip the soul and tear apart,
In shadows deep, you softly glide,
Tormenting hearts, where secrets hide.

You promise joy with a fleeting glance,
Yet leave behind a burning dance,
Your touch, a fire that sears the night,
Leaving hearts in relentless plight.

You whisper dreams, just out of grasp,
A haunting specter, a relentless gasp,
In the quiet hours, you twist and twine,
A tormenting ache, a bitter wine.

Oh, Desire, you cruel and cunning sprite,
Playing with hearts in the dead of night,
Your allure, a cruel and wistful dance,
Leaves scars upon the soul's expanse.

In your embrace, hope and pain collide,
A tumultuous tide, where hearts abide,
Forever elusive, your grip unkind,
Oh, Desire, tormentor of the mind.

The Deception of Hate

Hate, with her seductive guise,
She whispers comfort, feeds our lies,
But beneath her cloak of night,
She blinds our souls with vicious spite.

A charade of solace, a venomous dance,
She lures us in with false romance,
Turning hearts cold, inflicting pain,
Leaving scars, a relentless stain.

We drink her poison, unaware,
Thinking vengeance is just and fair,
But in the end, we're left to see,
It's ourselves we've bound in misery.

Oh, Hate, a cruel and bitter foe,
Her embrace a facade, we now know,
For she devours hearts with glee,
Leaving us empty, longing to be free.

Anger's Paradox

Anger, my fierce and fickle friend,
You surge when wounds refuse to mend,
Born of hurt, ignited by pain,
A tempest unleashed, both loss and gain.

You shield me from injustice's sting,
Yet leave remorse in your fiery ring,
I hate you for the havoc you sow,
Yet you're the first to shield my woe.

In your embrace, I find release,
A bitter solace, a troubled peace,
Oh, Anger, you know me too well,
In your fury, my heart's bitter swell.

Your love is fierce, your grip is tight,
Yet in your wake, regrets ignite,
For when you fade, the scars remain,
A bitter truth in your relentless reign.

Sanctuary of Solace

Amidst the cyclone of meetings and heat,
Where stress and weariness find their seat,
Friday arrives, a heavy cloak unfurled,
Weary bones ache in the relentless world.

Seeking solace in a cool, soothing bath,
With creamy scrub and soap's soft path,
Immersed, tension starts to release,
Music soothes, offering inner peace.

Pampered tresses and scented soap,
A divine ritual to cleanse and cope,
As muscles relax in the cooling wave,
Stress dissolves, peace engraves.

Each breath deepens, tensions abate,
In this sacred pause, time and fate,
Emerging renewed, burdens shed,
Mind clear, spirit light, heart stead.

Ode to Garlic

Oh, garlic, pungent and bold,
In my heart, your charm takes hold,
Pickled by my mother's hand,
You're a delicacy, oh so grand.

If garlic were a man, I'd say,
I'd marry him without delay,
For your flavor, I'm so smitten,
In dishes, you're always hidden.

Your scent lingers, strong and true,
Yet I can't resist, I love you,
In stews, in sauces, roasted fine,
You make every dish divine.

Oh, garlic, my culinary bliss,
In my world, you're not to miss,
If you were a man, it's true,
I'd marry you, no one but you!

A Moment's Glance

Each day unfolds, a silent plea,
For just one look, a glance from thee,
My heart in knots, my soul aglow,
Yearning for a glimpse, a tender show.

In shadows cast, I stand and wait,
Hoping our eyes will soon relate,
Time crawls by in endless spin,
As I ache within, longing to begin.

Your eyes, a beacon, distant and fair,
Hold the essence of love laid bare,
Yet your gaze, a distant shore,
Leaves me longing, craving more.

Oh, how I pine for that fleeting sight,
To bask in warmth, in your light,
In your glance, my world complete,
A love so pure, so bittersweet.

For in your eyes, I find my grace,
A moment's glance, my saving place.

Elegy of Love

In twilight's hush, memories unfold,
Of love once vibrant, now growing cold.
Promises scattered like autumn leaves,
As our hearts learn how to grieve.

Your smile, once bright as morning light,
Now a fading star in the vault of night.
Recollections linger, bittersweet and bare,
A love worn thin by time's wear.

In solitude, your absence looms,
A chasm widening in empty rooms.
Adrift in the wake of what might have been,
At crossroads, unsure how to begin.

Warmth has fled our once-shared space,
Leaving only shadows in its place.
Our passion's tale, now tinged with rue,
Dims like twilight losing its hue.

Yet in this ache, your memory stays,
A gentle refrain of bygone days.

Sara Mhatre

Hello, Myself Sara Mhatre from Mumbai, Maharashtra, India. I am 18-year-old girl trying my luck into creative writings to keep myself motivated and creative for a long time.

To be very honest, Writing is my IKIGAI. It's the purpose of my life. The only hobby that I love doing, the world might need. It really keeps me happy and motivated.

Most of my poems are actually written by the girl that was deeply and madly in love with someone.
I hope you like my small 12 poems in the book.

With love,
Sara <3

New Year's Eve

It was Sunday evening
The sky was Orange
The sun was ready to set
Meanwhile the moonlight already started the play

There comes a silly girl
Who always had fond of the moon
Started to dance Carefree
Even though the evening was cool

Birds were chirping
Singing their song
The girl was enjoying
While dancing along

Slowly the stars
Came to the show
They were so bright
The room began to glow

That's how the girl
Was enjoying her night
All Alone
Joyfully and Quiet.

The Moon of My Life

He was the moon of my life,
Who i adored from afar,
I was just another person for him;
Who was falling apart.

The Seasonal Love Story

Started the journey in the monsoon
When I didn't even know the meaning of autumn
I loved him like winters love snow
He took away my season spring
And left me in the forever fall

मेरा चमकता चांद

उसे हकीकत मे अंधेका करना उत्ना ही
मुश्किल है जितना अंधेरी रात मे चमकते चांद को अंदेखा करना

उसे देखु तो नाझरे हट्ठाने का मन नही करता
ना देखू तो हसने का मन नाही करता

चाहने वाले तो बोहोत हे उसके लेकीन समझ किसीको नाही आता
भोली शकल मे उल्झा लेता है सबको लेकीन हाथ किसी के नही आता

माना बकियो की तरह कमिया भी है उसमे
लेकीन बिना दाग के तो चांद भी खूबसुरत नाही लागता

Judgemental World

Being real made me mean
Talking with others made me noisy
Staying alone...oh she must be sad
Happily enjoying..oh she is so mad..!!!

Mean, Noisy, Sad or Mad;
Crazy, Idiot, Cool or Fool;
I can't hear you..!!!
I don't fear you..!!!

Call it what you want,
It's my life, it's my reputation
You are nobody to judge me
For being real..!!!

Oh no! I Am Falling In Love Again

I thought I was falling out of it
Thinking I won't see him again

Saw him being himself tonight
Shining like the shadowy moon
In the cloudy environment

It was difficult to unsee him
He was so cutely elegant
I think...it was meant for me
That I ended up falling again!

The Look of Love

Deeper than the ocean,
Prettier than skies,
Beautiful as the Rainbow,
And as elegant as birds in hives.

I was lost in him,
When he was busy enjoying life,
Did he ever notice my shiny eyes;
Whenever we meet??

Was that affection?
Or just an attraction?
That surely wasn't lust...
'cause it was clearly the look of love!!

Shayad

Shayad kuch tha apne beech
Shayad tum samajh nhi paaye
Shayad maine tumhe hadd se jyada chaha
Aur shaayad tum mujhe dobara tod gaaye

Shayad bohot si kamiya thi mujhme
Yaa shayad tum kaafi ache the mere liye
Shayad maine he dil thamaya usko
Jiskne shayad apna dil thamaya tha kisi aur ko

Shayad tumne mujhe do pal ki khushi deni chahi
Par shayad mei wo samjh naa paayi
Shayad maine aapse kaafi umeedein lagayi
Par shayad tumne usse kabhi nibhani nhi chahi

Shayad tumhe paana meri kismat mei nahi
Yaa shayad mujhe meri kismat par yakeen nhi
Shayad tumhe mere mohabbat par aitbaar nhi
Yaa shayaad mere mohabbat mei he koi kami reh gayi.

The Ocean and It's Flood

Time stopped when I was sunk in the ocean of love,
Not a log was there to hold onto,
Felt like forever as time passed in it
8 years and I was still swimming for him.

Daylight or moonlit,
Love and Respect played a war in there,
One wanted him,
Whereas the other one craved me!

Later, when I chose myself,
A Flood of memories, just flew across my mind
Wondering if he thinks about me or not?
Is it just me who's trying to swim across this ocean
Or has he already reached the shore of peace?

The War of Thoughts

I was so lost,
In my own thoughts;
Wandering around in the frost..
Thinking about someone's quotes.

It's been ages and I accept,
I still like him a lot;
As ignoring him is really difficult
Yet, his one soft smile still melts my heart

Rejection and acceptance
Always played a part
It's tough to walk on this strange path
But will he ever care if someday I just fall apart?

A Different Breeze

There's something different
Some kind of breeze
Something good, something new
Why is it bothering me???

A broken wing still
An angelic spirit
A different new hope
Is this the beginning of a new journey???

The question remained unanswered
The brain was in a rush to find them
And the heart remained silent as
TIME was gonna reveal everything!!!

I Tried & Now I am Tired

You can't say I didn't tried,
I lost myself to win you.

You can't say I didn't tried,
I damaged myself to fix you.

You can't say I didn't tried,
I went through sleepless nights
Crying for you; crying over you.

You can't say I didn't tried,
When all I ever wanted in my life was you.

But honestly now I done with this game;
Where you run & I chase!!!

Even if I catch you,
You won't stay.

Then why to play this game
Where, you run & I chase??

www.ingramcontent.com/pod-product-compliance
Lightning Source LLC
LaVergne TN
LVHW091058150826
845673LV00002B/627

9789364027939